LIVING WATER STUDY

HALEY SMITH

WestBow Press books may be ordered through booksellers or by contacting:

WestBow Press
A Division of Thomas Nelson & Zondervan
1663 Liberty Drive
Bloomington, IN 47403
www.westbowpress.com
844-714-3454

ISBN: 978-1-6642-1226-8 (sc)
ISBN: 978-1-6642-1227-5 (e)

Library of Congress Control Number: 2020922338

Print information available on the last page.

WestBow Press rev. date: 12/11/2020

WESTBOW
PRESS®
A DIVISION OF THOMAS NELSON
& ZONDERVAN

CONTENTS

BACKGROUND

My sophomore year in college, I started discovering a truth that needed further investigation. As I read through my Bible, in my own quiet moments with the Lord, I began to see a pattern. When water was mentioned in the Bible, it was *always* coupled with the power of God. I longed to find more verses that mentioned this *living* water. Over and over, I discovered that every time an object, person, or place encountered living water, transformation took place. Each time, it went beyond the natural. It was, and is, the natural linked together with the supernatural. Even more interesting is that this living water is not directly linked to Jesus until we reach the New Testament. It is there that Christ offers living water to the woman at the well. And it changes her. It changed me. It will change you. Through this study, we will explore the transformative power that comes when we allow the living water to enter our lives.

INTRODUCTION

Living water. What in the world does that mean? I had the privilege of traveling to Israel during my sophomore year of college. It was there that I saw a cold spring and wanted to drink from it. I was told I could but that the water was living. I was taken aback! Living water? Yes, water full of tiny organisms swimming and multiplying. I opted out of drinking this living water, but it got me thinking about the idea of living water. In order to get drinking water or clean/pure water, it has to be filtered. A process takes place where those living organisms can no longer get through. And after it goes through that process we are left with clean and pure water. It is this water that replenishes our physical body.

Although water is essential to our survival as a human, what we will be focusing on throughout this study is the living water that only Jesus offers. This is not the living water full of tiny organisms, but His transformative power. What would happen if we allowed this living water to fill us? For me personally, there have been times in my life where I could not see the light at the end of the tunnel. I was searching and seeking only to come up dry. But the living water that is sourced from Jesus filled me every time. There were times I was parched and thirsty, and the living water met my needs and brought life and light back to me. Are you thirsty? Do you feel dry and barren? Maybe you are dealing with a circumstance that is taking every ounce of your strength and is depleting you of your living water. Maybe you have no idea what I am talking about, but you know that there is a void that has not been filled no matter what you try to fill it with. Maybe you are at a place in your life where you can't get enough of the Lord. You want to go deeper, you want to be used, you want the living water to pierce every part of your life. No matter where you are at, living water is made available to you.

Through this study, we will investigate different passages that showcase the transformative power that comes when living water intersects with our lives. The focus will stem from John 4, and then we will dive into passages and scriptures from both the Old Testament and New Testament that refer to this living water Jesus speaks of. Are you ready to be filled? Come and drink from the well that will never run dry!

HOW THIS STUDY IS SET UP

Personal Study: There have been many times when I wanted to dive deep within a topic or a study but did not have the availability of doing a group study. This book is designed to be done as an individual study. However, it can be done within a small group setting. With this in mind, it is set up as a four-week, five-day study. Short enough to finish but deep enough to allow for reflection.

Foundational Passage: Throughout this study, John 4:7–38 will be our foundation, as within this passage the phrase *living water* explicitly refers to the Holy Spirit through Jesus for the first time. Week by week, keeping John 4 in the background, we will explore verses from both the Old and New Testaments that discuss life-changing qualities that come when we allow the living water to enter our lives.

Weekly Topic: Each week, we will explore a different topic. The topics are as follows: Salvation, Growth, Blessing, and At Last with God.

Intro Page: At the start of each week, there will be a weekly introduction to the topic. Within this page, you will find the intention of the week, the verse of the week, a prayer for the week, and a song of the week. I encourage you to play the song and let worship set the tone.

Scripture or Scripture Passage: Each day will have either a target scripture or a target scripture passage. So, pull out your Bible or your glowing Bible and get ready to dive in. If you are not familiar with the Bible or exploring verses, do not fear! The study is set up in a user-friendly and straightforward way.

Reflective Questions: Within each day of study are reflective questions. Some questions are simplistic, while others will cause you to think and reflect. Please allow yourself to go deep and answer the questions as truthfully and honestly as possible. The effort you put into this will equate with how much you get out of it. Let this book be your safe space where you can allow yourself to unpack and work through any emotions, circumstances, and feelings you may be carrying.

Weekly Takeaways: At the end of each week, you will have the opportunity to record your takeaways. This is a space created for you to write down the things you want to hold close and remember.

FOUNDATIONAL PASSAGE

JOHN 4:7–38

A woman from Samaria came to draw water. Jesus said to her, "Give me a drink." (For his disciples had gone away into the city to buy food.) The Samaritan woman said to him, "How is it that you, a Jew, ask for a drink from me, a woman of Samaria?" (For Jews have no dealings with Samaritans.) Jesus answered her, "If you knew the gift of God, and who it is that is saying to you, 'Give me a drink,' you would have asked him, and he would have given you living water." The woman said to him, "Sir, you have nothing to draw water with, and the well is deep. Where do you get that living water? Are you greater than our father Jacob? He gave us the well and drank from it himself, as did his sons and his livestock." Jesus said to her, "Everyone who drinks of this water will be thirsty again, but whoever drinks of the water that I will give him will never be thirsty again.[a] The water that I will give him will become in him a spring of water welling up to eternal life." The woman said to him, "Sir, give me this water, so that I will not be thirsty or have to come here to draw water."

Jesus said to her, "Go, call your husband, and come here." The woman answered him, "I have no husband." Jesus said to her, "You are right in saying, 'I have no husband'; for you have had five husbands, and the one you now have is not your husband. What you have said is true." The woman said to him, "Sir, I perceive that you are a prophet. Our fathers worshiped on this mountain, but you say that in Jerusalem is the place where people ought to worship." Jesus said to her, "Woman, believe me, the hour is coming when neither on this mountain nor in Jerusalem will you worship the Father. You worship what you do not know; we worship what we know, for salvation is from the Jews. But the hour is coming, and is now here, when the true worshipers will worship the Father in spirit and truth, for the Father is seeking such people to worship him. God is spirit, and those who worship him must worship in spirit and truth." The woman said to him, "I know that Messiah is coming (he who is called Christ). When he comes, he will tell us all things." Jesus said to her, "I who speak to you am he."

Just then his disciples came back. They marveled that he was talking with a woman, but no one said, "What do you seek?" or, "Why are you talking with her?" So the woman left her water jar and went away into town and said to the people, "Come, see a man who told me all that I ever did. Can this be the Christ?" They went out of the town and were coming to him.

Meanwhile the disciples were urging him, saying, "Rabbi, eat." But he said to them, "I have food to eat that you do not know about." So the disciples said to one another, "Has anyone brought him something to eat?" Jesus said to them, "My food is to do the will of him who sent me and to accomplish his work. Do you not say, 'There are yet four months, then comes the harvest'? Look, I tell you, lift up your eyes, and see that the fields are white for harvest. Already the one who reaps is receiving wages and gathering fruit for eternal life, so that sower and reaper may rejoice together. For here the saying holds true, 'One sows and another reaps.' I sent you to reap that for which you did not labor. Others have labored, and you have entered into their labor." (John 4:7–38 ESV)

WEEK 1:
Salvation

To kick off our study, we will be exploring the topic of salvation. This is our foundation. Salvation is our deliverance from the sins that entangle us and separate us from the Lord. It is because of Jesus and his death on the cross that this gift of salvation is offered to us. Yet death did not conquer Jesus. Rather, Jesus conquered death. We have salvation through Him. This week you will discover who has access to salvation, who Jesus is and who you are in Him, and our action steps within salvation.

Weekly intention:
The weekly intention is for you to understand what salvation is and the transformation that takes place when you accept the precious gift of salvation through the exploration and analysis of Scripture.

Verse of the Week:
John 4:10, "Jesus answered her, 'If you knew the gift of God and who it is that asks you for a drink, you would have asked him and he would have given you living water'" (NIV).

Song of the Week:
The song of the week is in Hebrew. On the next page, you will find the song in both the Hebrew translation and the translation of it in English. Spend time reflecting on this song.

Prayer:
Heavenly Father,

I praise you for you hold the heavens and earth in your hands. You are Almighty God, you are holy, and you are good. Thank you that your love came for me. You made a way for me to be restored and made whole. I accept your salvation that is made possible through Jesus. Let me walk in the power, love, and joy that salvation brings.

In your name,
Jesus,
I pray,
Amen.

Song of the Week

B'mayim zakim, Hu rochetz et raglai, Adonai, Elohai, Riboni,
B'ruach kodsho, M'male et ruche, Adonai, Elohai, Osi.
Damo hayakar, Hu shafach al nafshi, Mitzlavo haboded v'hanora,
Mayim chayim, Hu noten li lishtot, Adonai El Chai yeshua
Adonai El Chai Yeshua, Adonia El Chai Yeshua
With pure water He washes my feet—my Lord, my God, my Master. With His Holy Spirit He fills my spirit—my Lord, my God, my Maker. From His lonely and terrible cross He poured out His precious blood on my soul. He gives me living water to drink—The Lord, the living God, Yeshua.

Week 1: Day 1

Nothing like a Hebrew song to kick off week one!

As mentioned previously, I was able to visit Israel during my college years. While I experienced so many things, one of the best takeaways from my time there was getting to speak and sing in Hebrew. This meant learning and singing Hebrew songs (which was a slow process). Eventually, my team and I did well enough with the language that we could read the words and sing the tune. The songs in Hebrew are unlike any worship songs we have here in America. The closest I could compare a Hebrew song to would be a hymn or a psalm. They are composed as a simple verse, a passage, a prayer, or a cry, and they are put to music and sang aloud as a declarative. To worship in Hebrew is such an intimate experience with the Lord. What I love most about the song on the page before, is the fact that it declares God as the source of living water. In a simple and pure way, it showcases our need for this living water and the transformation that takes place when He enters. It is with this declaration of God as our Savior, salvation, and Lord that our study begins.

Before we get started, create your own definition for living water:

Let us take a look at Zechariah 13:1 (ESV): "On that day there shall be a fountain opened for the house of David and the inhabitants of Jerusalem, to cleanse them from sin and uncleanness."

In one sentence, write down what you think this verse is talking about.

_____

_____.

You may read this verse and think, *What in the world does it have to do with a Hebrew song declaring God as Lord and Savior?* Let's break this verse down.

This verse is a clear depiction and prophetic vision of Jesus. Read the verse again and answer the following questions:

What line did Jesus come from? _____

Where did Jesus do most of His ministry? _____

What promise does it state? _____

Jesus came from the house of David and did most of His ministry in Jerusalem. But look at the promise here. Not only does it hint at our Messiah, Jesus, but it declares Him as a "fountain opened." A fountain that would cleanse *the inhabitants* from sin and uncleanliness!

Who are the inhabitants? _____

The inhabitants refer to the Jews living in Jerusalem. However, we also must keep in mind that Jesus did not come just for the Jews but for the Gentiles as well. Thus, this *fountain* was going to be opened up and would cleanse *all* from sin. It is not a fountain that is closed off and hidden from sight. Rather, it is a fountain that is open, free, ready, and available. Jesus did not come for the select few or to just be a great prophet to learn from. He came openly and freely. He came because He loved *you*. And He is the fountain that is open for all and for all eternity. This right here is the Gospel. This declares how through Jesus we are washed with salvation! How amazing that even before Jesus steps onto the scene, there has already been talk and declaration that Jesus would come not just as a man or a prophet but as God in flesh, bringing salvation to the world.

What are some things in your life that have made you unclean?

-
-
-
-
-
-

As you filled out your responses, there may have been some anxiety or fear of sharing too deeply. If there ever was a safe place to share your intimate feelings and circumstances, it is on these pages. But do not look too long at those things that have made you unclean because over the next few weeks, we will be looking at and discovering the one who will cleanse you from those very things that have stained you.

A friend told me a story of how when she was little, she didn't understand fountains. She went on to say that she figured a fountain was linked to a hose and that soon enough the fountain would overflow, and the water would spill out everywhere! She would exclaim, "Someone needs to turn the hose off, or else the water is going to spill out!" Finally, someone took her aside to explain that the fountain was not connected to a hose and that the fountain would never overflow because the water in the fountain was constantly being brought up to create the appearance of a never-ending water supply.

I feel like sometimes we get caught up thinking that the water is going to spill out. That salvation is limited and there is not enough for you. The fountain of Jesus is a never-ending supply. Let that sink in. It will not run out; nor will it cause frustration. He does not get upset at you coming. In fact, He invites you to come. He sacrificed His life for that very reason. Do not fret. Come to the fountain that will cover your uncleanliness and bring refreshment to an area that has become dry.

Make a list of the things that you believe will come back to life or be covered and cleansed as we journey through this study. What are the things that you need living water for? What do you keep filling your jar with that is anything but living water? Write those things down as a starting point.

1.

2.

3.

4.

5.

Keep your list in mind as we journey through the next weeks together, and watch how God fills, covers, and replenishes each of those things.

As we close for today, write down a prayer of submission. It can be in any form. Recognize your need for a fountain that is *opened* up. Tell the Lord those things that you need to be cleansed of. Tell Him the things that have become dry. Tell Him how thankful you are for this salvation that has come to you!

Week 1: Day 2

Read John 7:25–44.

Who are the people mentioned in this passage?

_____

_____

How many times does Jesus speak in this passage (red words)?

_____

That's right. Jesus speaks only three times. Within a passage packed with characters, Jesus does not go on lengthy monologues; He speaks only three times.

What were the people confused about regarding Jesus?

_____

_____

_____

_____

As we can identify from the passage, the people surrounding Jesus were confused over who He really was. Was He just a good man? Was He a magician? Was He a great prophet? Was He really the Messiah? So many propositions. I think this is also true of today. From every avenue and direction, we are bombarded with so many choices. Meditate, chant, be one with the universe, complete these steps to reach peace, and so on. And really the question underlining all of those is, Who do you say Jesus is? Instead of leaving that as a rhetorical question, let us pause here to answer this question and to take it a step further—for your answer to this question will be the most important answer you will ever give.

Who do *you* say Jesus is?

_____.

Who do you describe yourself as?

_____.

Let us jump to Matthew 16:13–20.

In this passage, Jesus is talking with the disciples, His most trusted friends and closest companions. He asks them what people are saying about the Son of Man. The disciples shared with Jesus what others thought about Him, but He wanted to know what they came to believe.[1]

Who did others claim Jesus to be?

_____

_____

_____

What is Simon Peter's response?

_____

_____

_____

---

[1] Guzik, "Matthew 16."

Simon Peter answered the question by declaring Jesus to be the Son of the Living God! This was quite the revelation, as further down in verse 17, Jesus tells him that his answer was given to him by God the Father, rather than the world around him. Simon Peter unlocked the key of who Jesus is, the Son of the Living God, the Messiah. Simon Peter was one of Jesus' closest companions. He walked besides Him on long journey's, he talked with Him, he knew His character. It was over time that Peter and presumably the other disciples came to this conclusion.[2] He did not let the world shape or change that. As Spurgeon said, "Our Lord presupposes that his disciples would not have the same thoughts as 'men' had. They would not follow the spirit of the age, and shape their views by those of the 'cultured' persons of the period".[3] Now refer back to your answer. Have you let the world shape your identity of who Jesus is? How is your answer similar or different from that of the disciples?

_____

_____

_____

It is my greatest hope that through this study you come to discover Jesus as more than just a man and a great prophet. I hope you discover Him as He truly is—the living water, Son of God, the Messiah.

---

[2] Guzik, "Matthew 16."
[3] Guzik, "Matthew 16."

Week 1: Day 3

As we continue to dive deep within the wells of salvation, let us stop and reflect over the attributes of salvation. Look at this verse below:

> With joy you will draw water from the wells of salvation. (Isaiah 12:3 ESV)

Wells, to the people of Israel, were a source of life as water was rare. Here in Isaiah a beautiful picture of salvation is painted. Going back to our foundational passage, Jesus offers the woman water. But water that will quench every thirst. Water that will lead to eternal life. This verse in Isaiah, shows us that salvation is like a well we can return to and draw from. And each time, the waters of salvation will meet our need and quench our thirst. Moreover, it is a well that will never run dry.[4]

Salvation was made final and complete because of Jesus; but let us notice that with joy we can draw up the water of salvation. Salvation is not a burden or a heavy weight. Rather, it infuses our lives with levity and joy. When we pull water from the Lord's well of salvation there is no need to be down-hearted. For what we draw, is sourced in the Lord.[5]

Think about your walk with the Lord. Have you been receiving His salvation with joy or with a heaviness?

_____

In life there are many things that are heavy and even God tells us that in this world we will have troubles. However, when you come to accept the Lord's salvation the burdens of this life are no longer yours to carry and bear. For the Lord takes those burdens and replaces them with His love and joy.

Read Matthew 11:28–30.

Write down the attributes surrounding salvation:

_____

---

[4] Guzik, "Isaiah 12."
[5] Guzik, "Isaiah 12."

In Isaiah we saw that joy accompanies salvation and here in Matthew it reveals to us that Jesus will give us *rest*. Rest for our souls. On top of that, He is not exclusive with salvation but rather inclusive. "Come to me *all* who labor and are heavy laden, and I will give you rest" (Matthew 11:28 ESV).

What are some things that you have been carrying that are heavy?

1.

2.

3.

Before we continue, take some time to release these to Jesus. Declare and claim His name over each thing and let the salvation that has already been given to you, cover you.

Not only is salvation a place where our souls can find rest, but the source that it stems from is everlasting. The salvation Jesus offers us is pure and clean. It is *living water*. This is echoed in John 4:10, "Jesus answered her, 'If you knew the gift of God and who it is that asks you for a drink, you would have asked him and he would have given you living water'" (NIV). Jesus comes to her. To understand Jesus' character more, flip back over to Matthew 11 and read verse 29. What characteristics are used to describe Jesus?

1.

2.

Jesus does not condemn. For he is gentle and humble. These characteristics are showcased when Jesus approaches the woman at the well. He did not belittle her but came to her with grace. In the same way, he was ready and willing to provide for her living water. It was there at the well where the woman received her salvation, and she and her town were never the same again. His character remains the same today. He is coming to you with grace and gentleness. So come, recognize your Savior, and take up your salvation with *joy*.

Week 1: Day 4

Today we will reflect on a short and simple verse:

> I will lift up the cup of salvation and call on the name of the Lord. (Psalm 116:13 NIV)

What is the psalmist lifting up? _____

Although obvious, the psalmist is lifting up the cup of salvation. Pay attention to the verbiage in this verse. The psalmist is lifting. He is not accepting, sitting, waiting, running, or dying. He is *lifting*. This word is an action. It is purposeful.

If you could name a verb to describe your current state of being when coming to the Father, what would it be?

_____.

Look back to the verse. What is in the cup? _____.

Reflecting back to the woman at the well, although Jesus asked the woman for a drink, *He* offered her something that was better than any well water. And that was living water, salvation. Through Jesus we have been freely given the gift of salvation. But we must accept it. Jesus has already filled the cup with his salvation, and it is freely ours to take. We can partake of it and then joyously celebrate and praise the one who has so graciously filled it for us.[6] We see here the psalmist lifting up the cup of salvation. A clear declaration of his acceptance. He is receiving the salvation the Lord so graciously bestows on us. In fact his mere action of taking the cup was an act of worship and praise.[7]

Notice what he does next. He *calls*. Again, another action. He does not whisper, and he does not sit in silence; he calls out.

Whom does he call out to? _____

---
[6] Spurgeon, "Psalm 116:13."
[7] Spurgeon, "Psalm 116:13."

In Psalm 116:17, we see the purpose behind calling on the name of the Lord. It reads, "I will sacrifice a thank offering to you and call on the name of the Lord" (NIV). The psalmist realizes his salvation is from none other but the Lord and that receival of salvation elicits a response of thanksgiving and praise. It elicits worship to the name above all names, the Lord.

Receive the salvation of the Lord and recognize the one who offers us that sweet gift of salvation. Spend some time today calling on the name of the Lord. Do it in a way that reflects who you are in Christ. Sing a song of praise to Him. Dance, journal, pray, serve, and so forth.

Week 1: Day 5

Christ himself died for you. And that one death paid for your sins. He was not guilty, but he died for those who are guilty. He did this to bring you all to God. His body was killed, but he was made alive in the spirit. And in the spirit he went and preached to the spirits in prison. These were the spirits who refused to obey God long ago in the time of Noah. God was waiting patiently for them while Noah was building the boat. Only a few people—eight in all—were saved by water. That water is like baptism that now saves you—not the washing of dirt from the body, but the promise made to God from a good heart. And this is because Jesus Christ was raised from death. Now Jesus has gone into heaven and is at God's right side. He rules over angels, authorities, and powers. (1 Peter 3:18–22 ICB)

In this passage, we have such a striking picture of salvation, and we can see how, through salvation, God invites us into unity with Him for eternity. Let us break this passage down further.

- "Christ himself died for you. And that one death paid for your sins"
  (1 Peter 3:18a ICB).

For whom did Christ die? _____

What was the price? _____

Let that sink in. The only Son of God came and died for *you*. It is personal. He did not come for some or the elect but for you. You are of worth to God. He came and took on your sin—sin that deserved death. Because of Jesus, you are released from your debt. You are set free.

Take a moment to meditate on the fact that God came for you. How does that make you feel? What is your response?

_____

- "He was not guilty, but he died for those who are guilty. He did this bring you all to God. His body was killed, but he was made alive in the spirit" (1 Peter 3:18b ICB).

16

Was Jesus guilty or innocent? _____

Jesus was innocent. He was not up on the cross because of a crime He committed. Rather, He was on the cross because of the crimes *we* committed.

Why would He do this? _____

He did this in order that we could be united with God, the Father. Notice this connection. Jesus, who was united to God, now brought us, sinful humans, into direct unity with God. Through Jesus, we have access to the Father. Although Jesus died, He was resurrected by the power of the Holy Spirit. In just a few verses, we have experienced the inner workings of the Trinity. And guess what? *We have access.* The same power that raised Christ from the dead now lives in us!

The passage in 1 Peter 3 mentions a recognizable person in the Bible, Noah. If you are familiar with the story of Noah, you will know that God looked down on the earth and "saw how corrupt the earth had become, for all the people on earth had corrupted their ways" (Genesis 6:12 NIV). The people continued to live in disobedience and unbelief. The floodwaters washed away all of the sin and evil to usher in a fresh start.[8] All was destroyed except for Noah and his family members—the eight who were saved by water. Let us jump over to his story now.

Read Genesis 6:9.

What characteristics are used to describe Noah?

_____

_____

_____

---

[8] Guzik, "1 Peter 3."

What characteristics would others use to describe you?

_____

_____

_____

_____

_____

It was Noah's faithfulness that saved him and his family. God looked down and saw his heart. Noah lived amongst a people who lived in disobedience and unbelief toward God. Noah was unique in the fact that he did not let those around him affect or shake his faith in the Lord.[9] God did not notice those who were working hard for a promotion or trying to gain the most friends. Rather, he looked for those who, no matter what, remained faithful to Him.

Turning back to the passage in 1 Peter, what were Noah and his family saved by?

_____

The same water that brought a cleansing to the whole earth brought a personal cleansing to Noah and his family. This is the same water we have access to because of Jesus. It is the living water that, as the passage points out, cleanses us not only on the outside but also on the inside.

---

[9] Guzik, "Genesis 6."

Jesus came to cleanse us from the inside out. What is the "dirt" that needs to be washed off you?

-

-

-

-

Accept the cleansing that comes when we allow the waters of salvation to sweep over us.

Challenge:

Read Genesis 6–9:17.

Reflect on the faith of Noah and his family. Reflect on the goodness and grace of God found within this passage.

Week 1 Takeaways:

1. What is your biggest takeaway from Week 1?

2. What verse or passage of Scripture was most meaningful to you?

3. What does living water mean to you?

4. How does God's salvation change you?

5. What truth about God impacted you the most?

6. How can you practically apply what you learned this week into your day to day life?

_____

Notes:

WEEK 2:
Growth

Week two is centered around growth. This is not the physical growth of our bodies, but rather the growth within our relationship with the Lord. As believers, it is important that we continue to learn and grow. It is not enough to simply believe. That belief should take action. Our salvation is not based on actions, but if salvation truly changed us, others should be able to see that. This week, we will be discussing and diving into the scriptures to explore the topic of growth as a believer. Within life, we cannot step into who God has created us to be if we are not growing or taking steps of action.

Weekly intention:
The weekly intention is for you to choose daily to grow as a believer. To not remain stagnant, but to move deeper into the person God has created you and called you to be.

Verse of the Week:
"Lord, if it's you, tell me to come to you on the water" (Matthew14:28 NIV).

Song of the Week:
The song of the week is "Oceans" by Hillsong United. I encourage you to listen to the song and spend time in worship before each day.

Prayer:
Heavenly Father,

I praise you that you are the God who formed me in the womb. You created me and you have given me a purpose. You stand behind me and tell me in which way to go. May my feet remain on the path of the few. May my eyes be fixated on you rather than my circumstances. Help me to choose daily to step into obedience and trust.

In your name,
Jesus,
I pray,
Amen.

Week 2: Day 1

Let us begin in Psalm 1:

> Blessed is the man who does not walk in the counsel of the wicked or stand in the way of sinners or sit in the seat of mockers. But his delight is in the law of the Lord, and on his law he meditates day and night. *He is like a tree planted by streams of water, which yields its fruit in season and whose leaf does not wither. Whatever he does prospers.* Not so the wicked! They are like chaff that the wind blows away. Therefore, the wicked will not stand in the judgement, nor sinners in the assembly of the righteous. For the Lord watches over the way of the righteous, but the way of the wicked will perish. (Psalm 1 NIV)

I want you to read this psalm through again, this time paying attention to the image that is created. Notice the imagery the psalmist uses.

What picture emerges in your mind as you read through Psalm 1?

Here in Psalm 1, the psalmist describes the life of the one who is faithful and that of the one who is faithless.

What does the life of the faithful look like?

_____

What does the life of the faithless look like?

_____

This activity may have been different for you. However, when we read scripture there is so much more waiting for us to discover and learn if we truly focus on the words that are written. I love exploring the Psalms as David and the other Psalmists have packed the passages full of imagery. God is a creative God. Thus, really embrace the power of your imagination and take hold of those images that are produced.

Hold tight to the image you formed and created from Psalm 1. When our lives are connected and sourced in the Lord, our lives prosper—not because we earn it but because our source is connected to the Lord.

What path are you on? Are your roots connected to the mighty power and love of Jesus or to the commonalities and culture of the world?

_____

_____

Be specific, describing with your senses.

What does it look like?

What does it feel like?

What does it smell like?

What does it taste like?

What do you hear?

Your growth as a believer hinges on the source your roots are connected to.

Let's take a look at the life of the faithless. They walk in the counsel of the wicked. Now reading this, one can deduce that no one would want to walk in the counsel of the wicked. However, spend a minute to ponder the people you surround yourself with. I once heard a pastor say, "Show me your friends, and I'll show you your future." The counsel or the group of people closest to us matter. Analyze the people who are closest to you.

Are they people who encourage, inspire, and breathe life into you? Or are they people who are discouraging, manipulating, and life suckers?

I'm not saying to just up and ditch those people, but they should not be the people whom you walk closest with. Next, the life of the faithless does not delight in the Word of the Lord.

What do you take delight in?

_____

This is a question we need to ask ourselves constantly. We need to check where our delights lie. Is it in friendships? Wealth? Job status? Marital status? If our first delight is not in the Lord, then our roots cannot grow. Our prosperity is weakened.

However, the life of the faithful is described like a mighty tree planted next to streams of water. Let that image surround you today. The faithful are not weak, small, or feeble but rather *mighty*. The faithful are not a weed, or shrub, or twig but rather a *tree*. A tree that yields fruit, a tree that does not wither but prospers. However, the tree can only yield and be prosperous because its life source is connected to streams of water.

What is the source you are connected to?

Circle your response to the questions below:

Are you connected to the counsel of the *wise* or the *wicked*?

Are you connected to the way of *sinners/mockers* or the way of the *redeemed*?

Are you connected to the *law of the Lord* or the *law of the world*?

Are you connected to the *Word that brings life* or to *words that destroy*?

Take some time to reflect on these questions. As you reflect, don't let your heart become discouraged. Rather, let these questions spur you on to reconcile your relationship with the Lord and to rearrange your priorities. Look to Jesus our Savior and hold fast to the truth that the Lord watches over you. May your roots be sourced in the streams of the Lord, for whatever you do will prosper.

Week 2: Day 2

Read Exodus 17:1–7.

The Water from the Rock

To give you some context, both this passage and the passage further down fall within the Israelites' journey to the Promised Land. They had been under subjugation for four hundred years and set free by the Lord. Moses was their leader. Along their journey, the people became frustrated and in need of food and water. Naturally, they began complaining. They said, "Give us water to drink" (Exodus 17:2 NIV) and "Is the Lord among us or not?" (Exodus 17:7 NIV). They needed their physical needs met. In Exodus, Moses was at his wit's end and asked the Lord, "What am I to do with these people? They are almost ready to stone me" (Exodus 17:4 NIV). The people were so outraged and in need of water they were ready to stone their leader—the same leader who brought them out of captivity. *They let a temporary need dictate their circumstance.* They had forgotten in a time of need the faithfulness of the Lord.

What need are you letting dictate your circumstances around you? Are you letting it speak louder than the faithfulness of the Lord?

_____

It may be hard to differentiate between a need and a want. However, look back at the passage and notice the need of the Israelites. They *needed* water. Physically they could not survive long without it. It was out of their control. It was something that was impossible for them to meet. A need goes beyond a want, for that can be met in human strength. What need do you have that only the Lord can meet?

_____

In Exodus, the Lord responded to Moses, "I will stand there before you by the rock at Horeb. *Strike* the rock, and water will come out of it for the people to drink" (Exodus 17:6 NIV). God not only supplied and met their need when it seemed impossible, but He was also there to show them He had not left their side. This was a significant and generous miracle. When Moses struck the rock, water gushed forth. This miracle is also a foreshadowing of Jesus. For when Jesus was struck on the cross, His living water flowed out for all of us to receive in full.[10]

---

[10] Guzik, "Exodus 17."

Take your need to the feet of Jesus. Lay it down and drink from the rock.

Read Numbers 20:1–13.

Again, the Israelites found themselves in dire need of water. This time, they declared, "Why did you bring us up out of Egypt to this terrible place?" (Numbers 20:5 NIV). They, once again, lost sight of the Lord's faithfulness. God told Moses and Aaron (Moses's brother) to gather the people and *speak* to the rock, and water would gush forth. Can you imagine speaking to a rock and water coming out of it? Well, neither could Moses. For, again, the people were in need of water, and Moses remembered the time before when God told him to *strike* the rock and water would gush out. Moses did not believe that he could *speak* and water would come out, so instead he *struck* the rock as he did before. He doubted what God could do. He took the matter into his own hands. Now notice at the end of the passage water still flows forth. The people's need is met despite Moses's disobedience. However, because Moses did not obey, he and the people would pay for it. They would never set forth in the Promised Land. God is a faithful God. He will meet our needs despite our faithlessness, but our disobedience will cost us.

What is something you have taken into your own hands?

_____

What is something you stopped believing God could do?

_____

The Bible tells us, "For I know the plans I have for you, declares the Lord. Plans to prosper you and not harm you; plans to give you hope and a future" (Jeremiah 29:11 NIV). Notice it does not read, "For I know the plans I have for myself." God desires for us to grow in Him. But how can we if we keep taking back control?

What do you need to let go of and give God complete control over?

_____

Will you trust Him with your plans, hopes, and future?

_____

Surrender those to the Lord and allow Him to meet your needs.

Week 2: Day 3

Today we are going to look at what happens when we face obstacles on our path and the path we choose after facing those obstacles. Our growth as a follower of Jesus is contingent upon the path we continue to choose. Are we choosing to lift our eyes to Jesus and run after Him or are we choosing to place our hope and trust in ourselves?

Today we will be reading about Jeremiah. Jeremiah was a man who was chosen by God to be His spokesperson to the Israelites. In the first chapter of Jeremiah, God calls him and appoints him as a prophet. Turn to Jeremiah 1:6. What was Jeremiah's immediate response to God's call? _____

That's right. Jeremiah did not think he was capable due to his age and his inability to speak in front of large crowds. If anything, let this encourage you. Jeremiah did not view himself as a man qualified to do the work of the Lord. And yet God still chose him. Jeremiah's response was not an immediate "Yes Lord!" It was hesitant. I often feel that hesitation. Do you? What is something God has called you to, but you feel hesitant about? Why do you feel that way?

_____

Jeremiah's hesitations spoke into his identity. When God called Jeremiah, He said, "Before I formed you in the womb I knew you, before you were born I set you apart; I appointed you as a prophet to the nations" (Jer. 1:5 NIV). God Almighty called Jeremiah in an intimate way but also in a way that confirmed his true identity. Before he was even born, God knew him, and God set him apart for a purpose. And yet Jeremiah's response shows us that he was hesitant to fully step into the identity God had given him. God will always call you in the way He sees you, in the way you were designed. You are called to more. You are called to something greater than yourself. Somewhere along the line, Jeremiah let the lies from the enemy sneak in: "You are not good enough," "You are too young," "You stumble over your words," and so on. He was fixated on his weaknesses. Though our weaknesses may cause us to respond meekly, they should not thwart us from pursuing the call of God.[11] Do not let your weaknesses and insecurities form and shape your identity. For though Jeremiah protested, God's response was "you shall go" (Jeremiah 1:7). God would not let Jeremiah's hesitations keep him from

_____

11 Henry, "Jeremiah 1."

30

fulfilling the call to more.[12] What is shaping your identity? What are the lies you have believed from the enemy about who you are and what you are capable of? Write them down below, surrendering them at the feet of Jesus.

-

-

-

-

-

Once we can let go of the lies, we can see clearly that God always calls us to something greater than ourselves. We were created for more than we could possibly imagine. In order for growth to occur, we must believe this to be true and step into God's calling.

Once Jeremiah realized God called him and created him for more, he was able to step into the calling God placed upon his life. God used Jeremiah to speak to His people, the Israelites. Read the verses below:

> "My people have committed two sins: They have forsaken me, the spring of living water, and have dug their own cisterns, broken cisterns that cannot hold water." (Jeremiah 2:13 NIV)

> Lord, you are the hope of Israel; all who forsake you will be put to shame. Those who turn away from you will be written in the dust because they have forsaken the Lord, the spring of living water. (Jeremiah 17:13 NIV)

In both verses, there are commonalities. Let us explore a couple.

1. The Israelites forsook God.

---

[12] Guzik, "Jeremiah 1."

What does it mean to forsake something or someone?

_____

Forsake means to *abandon* or *leave*, to renounce or give up on something of value. For God to say this to His people meant they gave up on Him. And in turn, they left Him for something they deemed as better. In Jeremiah, you can read that the Israelites sought after idols. They believed these statues to be better gods than the Almighty God.

What are the two evils listed in Jeremiah 2:13?

1.

2.

What sort of cistern does the verse describe?

_____

Not only did they find a replacement god, but by "digging their own cisterns", they took matters into their own hands. They gave up on waiting for the Lord; thus they took it upon themselves to control their own paths. A cistern is a receptacle that is built to catch rainwater. Thus, it acts like a well. Ancient workers developed a sort of lime plaster that would ensure that water would not seep out of the bedrock. However, if a crack developed, the water would seep out, and it would become a broken cistern. The Israelites, choosing to worship idols instead of God, can be compared to that of a crack in one's cistern. Sure, the idols may have filled a temporary need for the Israelites, but it was not a place where water could remain. The idols could not fulfill their need. Only God, the spring of living water, can do that, which brings us to our next commonality.

2. God is the spring of living water.

Here in Jeremiah, God declares himself as the spring of living water. First, notice God did not say He was the cistern of plastered protected and sure water. No, He declared Himself as a spring. A spring is not man-made. It is a natural, never-ending source. The Israelites would have to continuously return back to their worthless idols time after time because they were a *limited* source. But not God. Our

God is *limitless*, and His spring will never run dry or become faulty. It is not rainwater. It is living and will fulfill and meet every need every time.

Today we talked about our identity in God. That He *always* calls us to more.

We also discovered that choosing our own path or chasing after anything that is not Christ is only a temporary fix. Our need can and will only be met through Christ, our Lord and precious Savior.

Just as with the Israelites, there is a choice and a call back to Jesus. But it requires you to turn away from your broken cistern and leave it forever behind.

What is something you need to leave behind but don't want to?

_____

_____

_____

This very thing that you wrote down has a hold on your life. Surrender it to Christ and allow Christ to fill that void. In addition, what is a practical way you can leave your cistern behind? Maybe it is a daily surrender. Maybe it is writing that thing on a notecard and finding a verse that declares the truth and power of Christ over that thing. Maybe it is writing it on a jar and smashing it as a visual and physical demonstration of your surrender and return to the fountain of living waters. Whatever it may be, make a personal application to the message learned from today.

_____

_____

_____

_____

_____

Week 2: Day 4

Our song of the week inspires our study for day 4. If you have not listened to the full song already, I encourage you to pause here and listen to the song in full. We are going to take a look at the passage where Jesus walks on the water. Now, maybe you are doing this study and thinking, *Here we go again! Another discussion surrounding this story from the Bible.* And I would not blame you for coming into today a bit jaded. Or maybe you have never read this passage and are thinking, *A man walking on water … utterly ridiculous!* Whatever viewpoint you come into today with, set it aside. I want us to look at this passage with fresh eyes, observing the importance of the water, but more importantly the growth that takes place within Peter. After all, the song "Oceans" is a forever favorite for a reason.

Let us begin by diving into the scriptures. **Read Matthew 14:22–33**.

This small snippet in the Bible takes place directly after the feeding of the five thousand, a miracle that the disciples not only witnessed but were key players in. They watched as Jesus blessed the two small fish and the five loaves of bread. As they passed the baskets out to the multitude of people, everyone was able to eat and be satisfied. They ate and were filled. And shortly after, Jesus had His men get into a boat and travel across the sea.

Read Matthew 14:23. What does Jesus do during this time?

_____

_____

_____

Jesus, the only Son of God, perfect and blameless in His ways, took the time to go and spend time with Jesus alone. Let us stop here and take in this valuable lesson. If Jesus needed to take time and sit in the presence of His Father, then so do we. This is a key step in our growth as believers. We need to set aside time to spend with the Father alone.

Challenge: I challenge you to schedule a time this week that you can spend alone with God. During that time, push away all the distractions and soak in every sacred moment you have.

Come back to this spot and record any takeaways from your personal time with the Lord:

[ ]

Now, back to the disciples. After witnessing this incredible miracle and watching each person be fed to their heart's and stomach's content, Jesus makes them get into a boat and begin the journey to their next location. They *trusted* Jesus, and they *obeyed* him.

In whom or in what is your trust rooted? _____

In verse 24, what was happening to the boat? _____

The waves flared up, and the boat was suffering. When I traveled to Israel, I was able to visit the lake that the disciples traversed across. While looking at it and taking it in, I was told that though the lake might seem calm, winds often rose out of nowhere and could topple a boat easily. Only skilled fishermen went out on this lake. And there were the disciples being buffeted by the waves.

Read Matthew 14:25. What time does Jesus go out to the disciples?

_____

Now hold on a second. The waves did not start on the fourth watch of the night. Rather, they started as evening came. The fourth watch of the night would have been anywhere from three to six o'clock in the morning! The disciples had been battling the wind and the waves all night!

How would you have felt in this moment of battling the winds and the waves?

_____

_____

After being bumped and pushed around, suddenly they looked up and saw a figure walking toward them. It was not a large wave but rather what looked to be a person! Put yourself into the disciples' wet shoes for a moment. Write down what your reaction would have been:

The disciples believed it to be a ghost and were filled with fear. Just hours before, they were bewildered and in awe of Jesus, but now, as they were struggling in a storm, fear swept in and overwhelmed their souls. Jesus saw their fear and said, "Take courage! It is I. Do not be afraid" (Matthew 14:27 NIV). He spoke directly into what they were experiencing and what they were feeling. Perhaps you feel like you have been struggling in a storm for a while now, and you feel as if your cries have not been heard. But, dear friend, look up. There is one who not only hears your cries but sees you as well. He is speaking to you, saying, "Take courage! It is I. Do not be afraid" (Matthew 14:27 NIV). Let these words of Jesus encourage your heart today.

Peter must have felt immediately more secure because his initial reaction to Jesus's words were, "Lord, if it's you, tell me to come to you on the water" (Matthew 14:28 NIV). I don't know about you, but that would not have been my first reaction to Jesus. Peter, however, a follower and close disciple to Jesus, wanted to be near Him once again.

What was Jesus's response in Matthew 14:29?

_____

_____

While the storm was still raging, Peter saw his Savior and desired to be with Him, despite the circumstances. And Jesus did not push Peter away. Rather, he told him to *come*. In the midst of your storm, Jesus desires you to come to Him.

Peter stepped out of the boat. Think about this pivotal moment. How full of anticipation and how fast his heart must have been beating as he stepped out to realize he was walking on the water in the direction of Jesus! Did the winds and the waves cease? No, but Peter, for a moment, was full of trust and obedience as he stepped on the seas that were raging. Although your circumstance may seem overwhelming, Jesus is sovereign over it. In fact, it does not shake Him. Notice that nowhere do we see in the passage that the waves and winds overwhelmed Jesus. And when Peter stepped out of the boat and walked on the water, the waves and the winds did not at first overwhelm him either. He was able to step above the circumstance and step on top of it.

What circumstance or area in your life or in the life of someone around you do you need Jesus to walk on top of for you and with you?

_____

_____

It was only when Peter saw the wind and the waves that the fear swept in, both literally and figuratively. The waves swamped him, and he cried out, "Lord, save me!" (14:30 NIV). What changed? Peter, for a split second, took his eyes off Jesus and put his eyes on the circumstances around him. And the circumstances around him seemed too impossible. Fear crept in and overtook him. I believe this is what often happens to us as believers. We are keeping our eyes on Jesus, but as circumstances arise that seem a little too impossible, we struggle to see a way through and let fear sweep over us. Jesus does not let Peter drown. He immediately reaches out and catches him. However, he does tell Peter these words, "You of little faith. Why did you doubt?" (14:31 NIV). This may sound harsh, but with his eyes fixed on Jesus, he was able to step above his fear through faith and trust. But when he took his eyes off Jesus, fear won. His faith was immediately diminished when he looked at his circumstance outside of Jesus. Do not doubt what Jesus can do. He is the one who can make the impossible possible.

What is causing you to doubt the power of Jesus in your circumstance?

_____

_____

For Peter, it was the overwhelming size and stature of the wind and the waves.

No matter the size, no matter how crazy or impossible what you are walking through or what is surrounding you is, it is nothing compared to the power and might of Jesus. The story ends as Jesus and Peter climb back inside the boat and the winds die down. The whole time on the water, the winds kept roaring violently. But once inside the boat, the sea and the wind were silenced. Jesus has the power to silence the wind in your life. But He must step inside the boat with you. In order to grow, we must lay down the control we think we have. We must surrender what we think should happen. We must trust and obey. I know this may sound simple compared to the situation you may be going through, but let it stick with you. Jesus never once faltered on the water. He never was shaken by the circumstance the disciples were in. And He will never be shaken by anything you are facing. He came to the disciples and met them in the storm. He is coming to meet you in your storm. Will you walk out to Jesus and trust Him?

Week 2: Day 5

We just read and learned about what it looks like when our feet are aligned with Jesus. Today we are going to finish off this week of growth looking in two different books of the Bible. We will be stopping in Psalms and in Isaiah.

Open your Bible and read Psalm 23.

I want you to take some time and really reflect on each word that is spoken here. Analyze this passage through your senses. What are you experiencing as you read this? What emotions does it stir up in your soul? What is your initial response?

Record the answers to these questions here:

Just six verses yet six powerful verses. Together we will explore verses one through four. In verse 1, David tells us that in God we lack nothing. Why? Because Jesus is our Shepherd. Now David was a shepherd himself. He saw this connection in a very practical way. In today's world, it can be hard to make the connection, but think about it. If there is a flock of sheep that is led and cared for by a shepherd, the sheep do not need to do much. The shepherd does all the work. The shepherd guides them, protects them, and feeds them. They need only to continue to follow him at the sound of his voice. With Christ as our Shepherd, we have an "assured dependence"[13] to Him. We need only to continue to walk at the sound of His voice.

---

13 Spurgeon, "Psalm 23:1."

Let us continue to verses 2 and 3:

He makes me lie down in green pastures, he leads me beside quiet waters, he refreshes my soul. He guides me along the right paths for his name's sake. (Psalm 23:2–3 NIV)

Circle the verbs in the verses above. These verbs show not only action but a sense of sovereignty and protection. As you continue along with Jesus, know that He desires the best for you. You are His. And He is yours. When all seems chaotic and loud around you, *He is there to make you lie down in pastures that are green*. Why include the color of the grass? To ensure us that our Shepherd is not leading us to just any pasture but one that is lush and growing and flourishing. *He will lead you beside quiet waters*. Remember from yesterday that as soon as Jesus entered the boat, the winds died down and the water settled. The key word here is *quiet*. The disciples were tossed and tumbled by waves that were loud and aggressive. But as soon as Jesus came in the boat with them, all was stilled. *Our soul becomes refreshed in Him*. Think back to the woman at the well. Her thirst could never be quenched by water. Nor could she receive any sort of refreshment from it that would last. But the living water, Jesus, will quench any thirst and will refresh our souls. Next, *he guides*. Using the verses written out above, where does he guide us? _____

Have you ever found yourself on the wrong path? I know I sure have. And it is usually when I am following my own plans or trying to manage in my own strength that I wander and begin trekking down the wrong way. But our Shepherd will not only put our feet on the right path but will guide us there! How reassuring! Before we continue, I want us to pause and complete an activity. I pointed out the four verbs that David used to describe the actions the Lord will complete in our lives. I want you to think about your life and where God has you in this season. Think about a word you want to declare over your life. Next, write down the word in action form. For example, right now you may be overwhelmed with anxiety, and the word you can declare over your life in this very moment is *peace*. Now turn it into an action: Jesus will calm my anxious heart. Once you have some words and action phrases written down, look up a passage of scripture that can be directly linked to those words. This way, you can know that not only will God provide the action, His Word has already declared it to be true.

Word	Action Phrase	Scripture

Moving forward, read verse four.

> Even though I walk through the darkest valley, I will fear no evil, for you are with me; your rod and staff, they comfort me. (Psalm 23:4 NIV)

David did not use a particularly strong verb here. He uses the verb *walk*. Now I do not know about you, but if I was facing the darkest valley or a traumatizing event, I would not want to walk, but rather run! And David is not simply referring to a moment when he was *in* a dark valley (or as other translations put it, the valley of death), but rather when he walked *through* a dark valley. Although the Lord guides us and refreshes us, we will face dark valleys. Valleys that overtake us. Valleys that we can't run through but must walk through. Though our natural instinct may desire to flee, the Lord walks besides us. That was David's secret. Even in a worst-case situation or circumstance, David held onto the truth that God was with him. Remember Jesus is our Shepherd. His rod and staff will guide you and comfort you. No matter what you are facing, God is with you. With this in mind we can advance steadily rather than in a frenzied state.[14]

---

[14] Spurgeon, "Psalm 23:4."

Challenge: Read through and meditate on the remaining two verses of Psalm 23. Let the truth of God fill your heart.

Read Isaiah 49:10 (NIV) below.

> They will neither hunger or thirst, nor will the desert heat or the sun beat down on them. He who has compassion on them will guide them and lead them beside springs of water.

Do you see and feel the connection here? This passage is within the context of God leading and guiding the Israelites out of exile and to Judah, but also that of when God gathers His people in the last days. The journey for the Israelites was *long.* And they were in the desert. We already observed that the Israelites would complain often, but God met and supplied their needs tenfold. Who could forget the water gushing from the rock? But even more than meeting his people's physical needs, God also supplied their spiritual needs. God also has supplied our spiritual needs. For through the sacrifice of Jesus, our thirst for eternity is quenched. And in our last days, we will not be in need, for Jesus will guide us and lead us into eternity with Him. Continue to choose to walk alongside Jesus. Continue to choose to listen to His guidance.

Week 2 Takeaways:

1. What is your biggest takeaway from Week 2?

2. What verse or passage of Scripture was most meaningful to you?

3. Why is growth so important in our relationship with the Lord?

4. What truth about God impacted you the most?

5. How can you practically apply what you learned this week into your day to day life?

_____

Notes:

WEEK 3:

Blessing

Welcome to week 3! This week, we will be looking at the blessings of the Lord and how God does not just promise to bless us, but He always blesses us in abundance. This abundance of blessings can then overflow so that we may give to others. As you walk through this week, be mindful of the blessings God has already bestowed upon you and reflect on their nature. Were they stagnant? Were they small? Were they beyond what you could have ever imagined? Reflect on why this may be so. This week should draw us closer to the nature of the Father's heart. On the next page you will find a blessings list to record active blessings the Lord has bestowed on you. In this regard, you can see the activity of God in your life.

Weekly intention:
The weekly intention is for you to understand how and why God blesses those who love Him and how those blessings affect us and our relationship with the Lord.

Verse of the Week:
"They gave Moses this account: 'We went into the land to which you sent us, and it does flow with milk and honey! Here is its fruit" (Numbers 13:27 NIV).

Song of the Week:
The song of the week is "From Whom all Blessing Flow" by Hillsong United. I encourage you to listen to the song and spend time in worship each day.

Prayer:
Heavenly Father,

I praise you that you are the God who blesses in abundance. You provide for my every need. You remain faithful even when I am faithless. God increase my faith, that I may encounter more of you. Help me to be a blessing to those around me.

In your name,
Jesus,
I pray,
Amen.

Blessings List

This is a space for you to record the blessings that God has given you. Record the day it happened and what the blessing was.

Date	Blessing	Praise

Week 3: Day 1

Read Isaiah 55.

Who is the invitation for? _____

Who would be considered the thirsty? _____.

I wanted us to begin here so we can reflect on the simple invitation and blessing of salvation that we studied in week 1. We cannot overlook this. Here in Isaiah 55, the invitation is for the thirsty. The thirsty refers to all. It refers to you and me and your neighbor across the street.

What is the command to the thirsty?

_____

_____

_____

God simply tells us to come. To come broken and wounded. To come lost and searching. To come down-hearted. To come as you are. He does not ask for money or anything in return. We can come with confidence and faith in Him.[15] He simply wants us to come and to take our fill. To be filled and overflowing with the salvation that is made possible from Jesus.

Read Isaiah 55:9–11.

What do rain and snow provide for the earth? _____

Although rainy days may seem gloomy, they bring hope of life, for the rain waters the earth so that the earth may flourish. Notice in verse 11, the Word of the Lord goes out, but it does not return void. Rather, it will accomplish the Lord's purpose. What is that purpose? For good!

---

15 Guzik, "Isaiah 55."

What has been keeping you from coming as you are? What has been keeping you from trusting the Word of the Lord?

_____

_____

_____

_____

_____

_____

Take these things to the Lord and hold onto the blessing that is stated in verse 12, "You will go out in joy and be led forth in peace" (NIV). This blessing will be not for our own renown but for the Lord's renown. I leave you today as you go out in joy and are led forth in peace.

Week 3: Day 2

The Overflowing Blessings of the Israelites

Buckle your seat belts, as today and tomorrow we will explore one of the greatest blessings discussed and showcased within the Bible, the Promised Land. If you are not familiar with this particular blessing, not a problem, as today we will be exploring several passages in the scripture regarding it. However, to give you some context before we start, the Promised Land was the land the Lord promised and set aside for His chosen people, it was a land *flowing with milk and honey.* (Side note: This will be a phrase we will explore together later but one that is important to remember.) God was going to give the people back their own land. For before Moses came and helped rescue them out of slavery, they were under extreme brutality from the Egyptians. This Promised Land was for them.

As we begin, what image comes into your mind when you read the phrase *"a land flowing with milk and honey"* (Exodus 3:8 NIV)? Draw the image that you see, or simply describe it with words in the box below.

```



```

Read Exodus 3:7–10.

What did the Lord see? _____

What was His feeling toward the Israelites' suffering?

_____

What was the Lord going to do?

_____

I wanted you to answer these questions in order to reveal the closeness of God in the Israelites' lives. God was not unaware of what the people were going through. Rather, He had *seen* their suffering and *heard* their cries. Let that sink in. God is not far away from our sufferings but rather in the midst of them. Though He is separate, He hears us and sees us.[16] He notices the details. The scripture here tells us that God was *concerned*. What does this reveal to you about God's character?

God planned on rescuing His people, and to do that, He would move them out of slavery and brutality and bring them back to their land.

List the words used to describe this land (3:8):

-

-

-

-

-

Look at the words you wrote from the list above. What word resonates the most with you? Circle that word. I want you to keep that word in your mind. For me, the word that resonated most was *good*. God promised the Israelites a *good* land. Not one that was bad or full of traps and tricks. This reveals to me more of who God is. He is a good and gracious God, bestowing upon me goodness. The phrase I had you draw out at the start is also found in this description of the land. *A land flowing with milk and honey.* What does this mean? Look back at the picture that you drew. God used this phrase to give the people and Moses (their leader) a visual picture they could hold onto. It represents a land that is bountiful, one that exudes splendor and productivity. God was not leading them to a land that was barren or deserted but rather one that was bursting with life! However, let us take a look at the end of

---

[16] Guzik, "Exodus 3."

verse eight. This land was occupied with multiple people groups living there. Why do you think God would send them back to their land with it already occupied? _____

Although this land was already given and claimed by God for the Israelites, they would still face challenges. The main challenge the Israelites faced was conquering these people groups and establishing their land under the sole authority of God. God gave them the land, but they had to work and fight for it.

Think about it in terms of your areas of expertise and skill. For example, I am a special education teacher. I love what I do, and I know God has called me to that field. However, it is not always a walk in the park. Every day, I must work and fight hard for my students. I have to learn and grow in my field. I work hard and give it my all because it is the field and land God gave to me in this season. I do this not for personal gains but to glorify God where He has placed me. Are you willing to work and fight for the land that God has given you? Why or why not? If not, what is keeping you from defending and maintaining your land?

_____

_____

_____

_____

_____

_____

Just as God promised the Israelites a land flowing with milk and honey, so too has He given you a Promised Land. However, whether we view it as a land flowing with milk and honey is up to us. We can walk forward into our land, or we can stay wandering in the wilderness. Stepping forward will not always be easy, but remember the Lord goes before us and is with us every step of the way.

Week 3: Day 3

Yesterday, we took a look in Exodus as God promised the people a bountiful land. Today we will look at the Israelites' reaction to their blessing.

Read Numbers 13:17–33

Men were sent to explore and gather information about the land for forty days. They went, explored, and gathered. Looking at Numbers 13:27–29, record the report given by the men in your own words:

_____

_____

_____

_____

_____

What was the overarching emotion of their report? _____

The men saw that the land was indeed bountiful and rich with produce and life. They rejoiced in that. However, there was an exception. Although they saw that the land was good, there was an obstacle. What was that obstacle?

_____

Overall, the people were afraid. They let fear and doubt sink in. They forgot that God had declared this land theirs. They forgot that the Lord was with them. But, not all of the explorers were filled with fear. In fact, take a look at Numbers 13:30, "Then Caleb silenced the people before Moses and said, 'We should go up and take possession of the land, for we can certainly do it'" (NIV). This should have been the majority's response. After all, God had been with them this whole time. Caleb saw that even though there were enemies to defeat and conquer, they would not be alone. He responded out of trust and obedience.[17] He fully stepped into the land, knowing it was theirs for the taking, because God had claimed it for them. As we continue to read to the end of chapter 13, we see that the men did not let Caleb's hope, confidence, and resolve win. Rather, they continued to spread a bad report among the people.

Put yourself in the shoes of the explorers. What would your reaction have been? Record it below:

_____

_____

_____

_____

Oftentimes in life, we are given opportunities. But within those opportunities, we get to decide how much of ourselves we will invest. Maybe for some of you, when the going gets tough or even looks tough, you back down and try to find an alternative way through. And maybe there are some of you who see the obstacle but still push forward. It is a choice, whether or not to step fully into whatever God has placed before us.

Reflecting on the passage, circle what type of person you are:

Explorer with a bad report.

Caleb with a good report.

I want you to reflect, not to shame you or boost your pride, but to reveal to you at this current moment your reaction. To be completely honest, I relate most with the explorer with the bad report. If I was part of the team, I would be chiming in about how large and overwhelming the enemies seemed. But rather than let this realization stop me from going further, I must use it as my catalyst to propel forward. If I back down when the going gets tough, then I am trusting in myself rather than in the Lord. If I back down when the going gets tough, then I am letting fear speak into my life rather than the

---

[17] Guzik, "Numbers 13."

truth of God. If I back down when the going gets tough, then I am losing sight that God has already given me the land. Use your reaction, as an explorer with a bad report, as a catalyst for change. Reflect on why that is your reaction and bring it before the Lord.

For those of you who are fighters, you have ambition and courage. However, there is a fine line between pushing forward in faith and pushing forward in self-capability. Be careful not to lean on your own understanding. Instead, lean on the understanding that comes from the Lord. He will guide you as you bravely step forward.

Read Numbers 14:1–9.

Look at verses 1–4. Write down what the people did and said:

_____

_____

_____

_____

Did the people want to move forward into the land given to them by the Lord, or did they want to return to the land where they were enslaved? _____

Why do you think the people responded this way?

_____

At the end of chapter 13, we saw that the explorers spread the bad report among the people like a virus. That bad report grew and grew until the people were ready to go back to the land where they were enslaved and treated like animals. It may be hard to believe that they would want to make that drastic choice, but when you are constantly hearing a bad report, that is what fills your mind and fuels you. What do you think the people's reaction would have been if Caleb's good report had been spread among the people?

_____

_____

_____

This is a powerful truth to unpack, and unfortunately, we cannot spend much time here. But I do not want you to miss it. What we hear and what we tell ourselves has a great impact upon our outlook and perspective. Strive to be the person who carries and speaks a good report rather than a bad report.

Moving on, jump back into Numbers 14 and read verses 5–9.

What did Moses and Aaron do? _____

What did Joshua and Caleb do? _____

Did Joshua and Caleb change their report? _____

The leaders and the two brave men were distraught. They knew with every fiber of their being that God had given the land to them. They had seen the faithfulness of the Lord throughout the entire journey and knew that God was still faithful and by their side. And yet the people would not go because of fear. They gave into their fear and doubt which led to conscious betrayal of the Lord's goodness.[18] Unfortunately for the Israelites, that generation would never see or step foot into the Promised Land. Only Caleb and Joshua would enter and claim the land that they knew God had given them. They would experience the land flowing with milk and honey. Do not let fear allow you to miss out on the flowing abundance of the Lord. Rather, surrender the fear to the Lord and remind yourself of who God is.

Before we close out on today, I want you to make a list of the qualities of the Lord that you need to hold onto in order to continue to bravely step forward into all God has promised you. To make these qualities even stronger, find a verse that showcases the quality of God and try memorizing a few. That way, the next time you are faced with a choice to enter or retreat, you will be prepared with an arsenal of truths to combat the fear.

_____

[18] Guzik, "Numbers 14."

Quality of the Lord	Scripture Written Out	Memorized

Week 3: Day 4

Today we will explore a blessing that came to a widow and her sons.

Read 2 Kings 4:1–7.

What happened to the woman and her sons? _____

What was the problem she now faced? _____

"Your servant has nothing there at all," she said, "expect a little oil." (2 Kings 4:2 NIV)

Circle the key words in the verse above that describe how the woman viewed her current situation. From the above verse, do you think the woman had hope she could keep her sons from being taken into slavery? *Yes* or *No*.

Why or why not? _____

I want us to fully recognize the woman's state of mind and the situation she found herself in. She was absolutely hopeless. She had lost her husband, and in those days, if you could not pay your debts, you often had to sell yourself or your family members into slavery as bankruptcy was not an option. Thus, your only choice was to give your children up as payment for your debts.[19] Not only that, but the woman's creditor was giving her no grace at all. Have you ever found yourself in a hopeless situation? Was your feeling similar to or different from what the woman felt? Explain below:

_____

_____

_____

_____

---

[19] Guzik, "2 Kings 4."

The woman had no hope, but Elisha did. He treated her with kindness and generosity when he asked, "How can I help you?" (2 Kings 4:2 NIV). It was a simple question but one that showcased the compassion and grace of Jesus. Look for areas in your life where you can utilize this simple but profound way to express the heart of Jesus to another.

Looking back at the passage, what did the woman have? _____

Even though the woman felt utterly hopeless, she was able to name at least *one* thing that she did have. If you are in a situation that seems bleak, I want you to write down at least one thing that you do have.

_____

If you are not facing a hopeless situation, record the things you have to be thankful for.

_____

Although small, the woman declared she had oil. Scholars believe this was not oil reserved for cooking, but a small amount of oil saved for the use of anointing.[20] This was a precious and sacred item. And it was this one item that allowed hope to enter into what was a seemingly hopeless situation.

What did Elisha tell the woman to do? _____

The blessing would not have occurred if not for the generosity and support of a community. The woman had to step out in faith and rely on the support and generosity of others. She had to exercise her faith in this manner. The blessing would not have occurred if she would have just sat there. Instead she had to activate her faith by stepping out and trusting that the Lord would supply and meet her needs.[21] Another important thing to note within Elisha's instruction was that she had to "go inside and shut the door behind you and your sons" (2 Kings 4:4 NIV). Why do you think Elisha had the woman go out to her community just to come back inside and shut the door?

_____

---

[20] Guzik, "2 Kings 4."
[21] Guzik, "2 Kings 4."

Although she needed the support of her community, the blessing did not come from them; nor was it meant to be public. Rather, in order to receive her blessing, she had to shut the door and experience it in private. This was more profound, as the woman personally and privately experienced a direct blessing from the Lord that drastically changed her and her family. God is a personal God. He sees us and will meet us in our need in a way that makes sense to us.

Read verses 5 and 6 again. What happened? _____

The woman and her sons listened and obeyed. They acquired the jars and poured and poured and poured until there were no jars left. God's blessing was related to her obedience and the size of her faith.

Activity

Below are several jars. I want you to fill in as many jars and to however high a level as you feel your faith is in your current season.

Reflect on your response. If you are in need of more faith, seek and pray to God to fill you. If you are full and/or overflowing, ask God how you can use that abundance of faith to serve others. In the end, the woman was able to use the oil to save her family. She was able to live off of the abundance of God's blessing. What seemed like a hopeless situation turned to one of hope, as God had done more than was thought possible.

Week 3: Day 5

You have made it to the last day of week 3! To close out of this week of blessing, we will be reading and looking in Psalms.

Read Psalm 65.

This is a psalm of thanksgiving for the many blessings of the Lord. There is a lot going on, so let us break it down. In verse 2, it says, "O you who hear prayer, to you all men will come" (NIV). As we have seen throughout this week and the previous weeks, God is not far from us. Rather, He is close, for He hears us. He is a personal God.[22] Think about a person in your life you can rely on for anything, a person you entrust your secrets and thoughts to. What causes this person to be trustworthy?

_____

_____

_____

_____

_____

God is like a close friend who listens. He hears you and sees you. But even more than that, He understands you.

Fill in these verses using Psalm 65.

"When we were _____ by _____, you _____ our transgressions. _____ are those you _____ and bring near to _____ in your courts! We are filled with the _____ things of your house, of your holy temple" (Psalm 65:3–4 NIV).

---

22 Spurgeon, "Psalm 65:2."

What sticks out to you most from these verses?

_____

_____

_____

_____

As we look further at those verses, we can see the transformation that comes into our lives because of Jesus. Through Him, our sins are forgiven. Sins that separate us from Him, he wipes away clean.[23] Through Him, we are united. In biblical times, only the Levites were allowed to enter the holy temple. However, when Jesus died, He died for all of us. In this verse, we get a glimpse of what that looks like. It is a blessing! God did not die for a select few but for all. And it is because of His death that we can approach Him not from far away but up close.

Reread verses 6–13. What do you notice about the second half of this psalm?

_____

In this remaining part of Psalm 65, David uses nature to showcase not only the beauty of nature but the characteristics of God.

List the attributes of God:

-

-

-

-

_____
23 Spurgeon, "Psalm 65:3."

Nature, as described in this psalm, exudes God's glory, power, beauty, strength, generosity, love, provision, and care.[24] If God takes care of the land, watering it and enriching it, how much more will He take care of you? If God crowns the year with bounty and overflows carts with abundance, how much more will He overflow His love to you? As you read the end of this psalm, I hope you were struck by the sheer abundance and fruitfulness that David describes in nature. David could have described the land as receiving just enough water to survive, or a few crops that were good, or even still streams half-filled with water. But David describes nature teeming with life and abundance. This is reflective of God's abundant generosity toward us. He is a good and gracious God. As God provides abundantly for nature, so too can we be thankful for His abundant blessings.

Create a list of the blessings in your life:

1.

2.

3.

4.

5.

---

[24] Spurgeon, "Psalm 65:6."

Looking over your list, are these blessings small? Or are they abundant and full?

_____

_____

_____

Spend time this week reflecting on the blessings God has given you. Praise Him for those blessings that are bursting with love, compassion, and generosity.

Week 3 Takeaways:

1. What is your biggest takeaway from Week 3?

2. What verse or passage of Scripture was most meaningful to you?

3. Why does God bless us?

4. What truth about God impacted you the most?

5. How can you practically apply what you learned this week into your day to day life?

_____

Notes:

WEEK 4:

At Last United with God

You have made it to the final week of our study! This week, we are going to explore passages that reflect on the promise that is waiting for us in eternity. These promises and truths belong to us as God's redeemed children. We will look at what our days will be like when we are at last united with God.

Weekly intention:
The weekly intention is for you to explore and reflect on the promise that awaits you in Heaven.

Verse of the Week:
"But our citizenship is in heaven. And we eagerly await a Savior from there, the Lord Jesus Christ, who, by the power that enables him to bring everything under his control, will transform our lowly bodies so that they will be like his glorious body" (Philippians 3:20 NIV).

Song of the Week:
The song of the week is "There is a Cloud" by Elevation Worship. I encourage you to start each day with worship.

Prayer:
Heavenly Father,

I praise you that you are the God who sits enthroned forever. You are holy and are due all honor and glory to your name. I eagerly await the day where I can be with you face to face. Until then, may I be faithful and obedient here on earth. May I bring good news to those around me. May I glorify your name.

In your name,
Jesus,
I pray,
Amen.

Week 4: Day 1

As we start this week, I want us to first get in the mind-set of heaven as our home. Recognizing our eternal home in heaven, is something we can find great solace in. When the world is chaotic around us, we know that our heavenly realm is still held together in perfect order. Later this week, we will read passages that link us back to the living water, but first let us turn to Philippians 3:20.

> But our citizenship is in heaven. And we eagerly await a Savior from there, the Lord Jesus Christ, who, by the power that enables him to bring everything under his control, will transform our lowly bodies so that they will be like his glorious body. (Philippians 3:20 NIV)

In the verse above, circle where our citizenship is held. Then, put a box around the word that describes our body before our transformation with Christ. Last, draw an arrow to the word that describes our body after being transformed by Christ. Just in this verse alone, we have seen that earth is not our eternal home. Rather, heaven is. This should cause a shift in the way we live.

Head over to **Hebrews 11:1–12**. This passage in scripture is often referred to as the "Hall of Faith". Within it we learn about various people who are commended and known for their faith. Read through these verses and discover the hall of famers for yourself.

In the following section, complete the chart using Hebrews 11. You will either record the person's name or will record what they were commended for. The first one is done for you.

Name:	Commended as or for:
Abel	Righteous man
Enoch	

Name:	Commended as or for:
	Heir of the righteous that comes by faith
Abraham	
Abraham and Sarah	

These amazing people lived lives that were bigger than themselves. These people all lived with a heaven mindset. They did not live for pleasures or wealth on earth, but rather lived in obedience to the voice and call of the Lord. Even to this day, they still have an impact on our lives, as we still recognize them as people of great faith.

To live in a way that is focused on our eternal home, our goal and mission must be aligned with that of Christ. Some of these people in Hebrews 11 never got to see the harvest of their work here on earth. However, it did not matter, for the promise was actualized in their faith.[25] They lived to make the world better. They lived to make the future better. And they did so by living how God created them to be.

What are you living for?

_____

_____

_____

_____

---

[25] Guzik, "Hebrews 11."

What do you want to be commended and known for?

_____

_____

_____

What are some practical things you can do to promote heaven's interests on earth?

_____

_____

_____

_____

Now read **Hebrews 11:13–16.**

What did these people admit about living on the earth? _____

What were they looking for? _____

Has God prepared that place for them? _____

He has prepared a city not only for them but for you as well. When we believe in the reality of God and His word then it allows us to believe in the reality of heaven.[26] Faith pushes past what is *real* or what can be seen and steps into what we cannot see. This week, we will explore what that city will look like and how that should spur us on while we live and breathe on the earth.

_____

[26] Guzik, "Hebrews 11."

Week 4: Day 2

Today we will explore the beauty and hope we have of living face to face within God's constant presence and how this affects us on earth and in heaven.

Read Psalm 84.

Here in Psalm 84, the author describes the longing to be within the courts of the Lord. All throughout the Bible, one can discover the various ways in which the Lord dwelt among His people. From the building of altars, to the tabernacle, to the temple, God's presence is always evident. In Jewish life, one way to be in the presence of God was visiting and making a pilgrimage to the temple. This was of high importance. In fact, people would take pilgrimages just to get there. Roads and places of refuge were constructed due to the large number of people who would travel to the temple.[27] The psalmist describes the blessing of simply being within the court of the Lord. Here he could stand in areas which were dedicated to glorifying the Lord. David's soul longed to be in God's presence.[28] What an even greater blessing we have! For we have the Holy Spirit that lives *within us*. In 1 Corinthians 3:16, we read, "Don't you know that you yourselves are God's temple and that God's Spirit dwells in your midst?" (NIV). As believers, we do not need to erect an altar or embark on a long journey to reach a tabernacle or temple. For His presence is within us.

Go through Psalm 84 again, this time writing down the way the psalmist describes the dwelling place or courts of the Lord:

-

-

-

-

---

[27] Spurgeon, "Psalm 84:1."
[28] Spurgeon, Psalm 84:2."

In Psalm 84:2, the psalmist declares, "My soul yearns, even faints, for the courts of the Lord; my heart and my flesh cry out for the living God" (NIV).

Underline the physical reaction the psalmist has to desiring to be in the courts of the Lord. Why do you think this is his response?

_____

_____

_____

Think about where you experience the presence of God. Perhaps it is in the car on your daily commute to work, in church, among a group of believers, or serving. Wherever it may be, visualize this place. What is your physical reaction to desiring to be in God's presence? Does your soul yearn? Does your heart cry out?

_____

_____

_____

Looking at your responses. Why did you record those answers? If you did not record an answer, why not?

_____

_____

_____

_____

The psalmist had a deep desire, a strong pull to be in the presence of the Lord. As believers and because of Jesus's death on the cross, we carry the presence of God with us, through the Holy Spirit. The psalmist did not have this access. However, I wanted us to see how great his desire was for the Lord's presence. On a scale between one and ten, how great is your desire to be in the presence of the Lord?

1   2   3   4   5   6   7   8   9   10

It is okay if your number that you circled is low or not where you want it to be. The Lord is faithful to increase your desire for intimacy with Him. Simply ask Him to increase your desire.

As believers, we are united with God through Jesus's sacrifice on the cross. If we do not desire to be in the presence of God, then how will others around us want to either?

Read Psalm 84:5–7 again.

Where do the people pass through? _____

What do they make it? _____

The Valley of Baka was either a real place or was used as a place to represent something. *Baka* in Hebrew means weeping. Thus, the people pass through a Valley of Weeping. Whether or not there actually was a valley with this name, we can all relate to a time in our lives where we or someone close to us passed through a Valley of Weeping. Notice, they do not keep it a Valley of Weeping for long. Instead, they transform it into a place of springs, a place overflowing with water. What is the importance of this? In their time of need and thirst, the very act of going to be in the presence of the Lord filled them with hope. So, even in a time of weeping, they were restored simply by the notion of being within God's presence.[29] How powerful! If you are in the Valley of Weeping, look forward. Continue on to be in the Lord's presence. Let Jesus shelter you and strengthen you along the way.

---

[29] Spurgeon, "Psalm 84:6."

In the presence of the Lord, we find shelter, favor, honor, and blessing. Fix your mind on the day when we will no longer have to "dwell in the tents of the wicked" (Psalm 84:10 NIV) but rather dwell with our Father in heaven for all of eternity!

Challenge: This week, look over your calendar and choose a few time slots to dedicate to being in the Lord's presence. These can be as short or as long as you want. Before those times, notice your body's reaction to desiring this set-aside time. Additionally, notice your reaction while in the presence of the Lord. At the end of your week reflect on these questions:

What effect did my time with the Lord have on me and my week?
What did God teach me or show me?
How did God's presence change me?
How did purposefully setting aside time to be with the Lord affect my relationship with Him?

Read Isaiah 35.

After reading, create a list of all the things that are declared to happen when the Lord returns for the redeemed.

-
-
-
-
-
-
-
-
-

Out of the list you just created, circle the ones that refer to creation. Put a box around the ones that refer to people.

Now that you have a nice list decorated with circles and boxes, let us take a look at what is happening to the land. In Isaiah 35, there is much imagery that showcases how wonderful and lush the land will be when the Lord returns. The land that was barren and parched will be glad, blossom, burst into bloom, and be full of life. It is as if nature will awaken and fully reveal God's magnificent glory.

Put a marker in Isaiah 35 and turn to **Romans 8:19–22**.

Here we see that creation is not fully displaying all of its glory. Rather, it is waiting, frustrated, and subjugated until the Lord returns. How odd to think about the fact that creation is not at its full capacity. The creation we see around us often takes our breath away. One of my favorite things to do is watch the mighty waves crash with significant force or stare up at the night sky to see millions upon millions of twinkling stars. And during these moments of observing and witnessing creation, I stand in awe of the Creator. Yet, creation is broken. It is trapped because of the brokenness of humanity. Though the earth and all of its creation is waiting under much groaning, when the Lord returns, the land will erupt in praise to reveal its full glory, pointing us directly to our Creator and Savior.[30] Look back up at your list and read over the words your circled. Notice the sheer joy and growth that will take place amongst the earth and creation. Where there is great lack, will soon erupt with fullness and majesty. Put a checkmark next to the areas of the earth that will be transformed upon the Lord's return:

_____ Desert   _____ Parched land   _____ Thirsty ground

_____ Wilderness   _____ Burning sand   _____ haunts of jackals

These are all areas of lack that need to be filled. What areas in your life are lacking, desperately needing and awaiting the touch and return of the Lord?

Those areas in your life will remain empty until they are surrendered to the Lord. Growth cannot take place if they are attached to the rules and subjugation of the world. Just like in Isaiah, those areas cannot burst forth in freedom and joy until the Lord comes. Surrender those places to the Lord and watch as He fills those areas with growth.

---

[30] Guzik, "Romans 8."

Now let us observe what happens to the people of the earth when the Lord returns. Flip back open to Isaiah 35 and reread verses 8–10. Who will be allowed to walk on the Way of Holiness? Who is not allowed to journey on it?

Allowed   Not Allowed

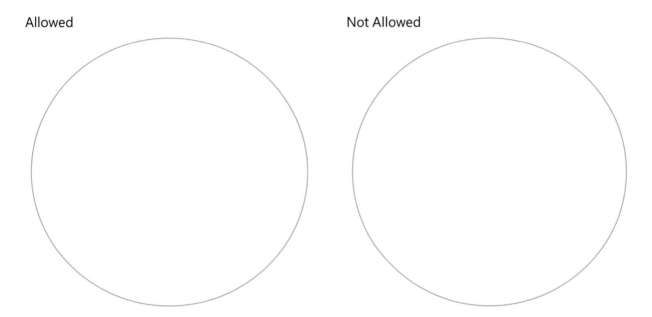

I do not know about you, but I want to be included in the bubble of people who are allowed. In order for me to be allowed, I must take into consideration the lesson we learned from week 1, that my salvation was made possible through the sacrifice of Jesus. Notice in Isaiah, the people the Lord has rescued will be allowed. Jesus did not come for a few but for all, including you. May you choose to receive God's free and overwhelming gift of love and mercy so that gladness will overtake you and sorrow and sighing will be rid of forever.

One last thing I want to point out is the connection between the land and people. The land and people are talked about interchangeably in this passage. Do not miss this connection. A pastor once shared that we are interconnected with creation. God created the earth in such a way that we are dependent on nature, and nature is dependent on us. For the very air we exhale is the air the plants take in. And the air the plants exhale is the air we need to live. God designed us to be in unity with his creation. In Isaiah 35, we get to see this picture brought to life. Not only will we be united with nature, but we will be united with our Savior.

Read Revelation 21:1–6.

After reading the passage, answer the following questions:

What did John see? _____

Where is God's dwelling place? _____

What will there be no more of? _____

Who does God declare Himself to be? _____

Who does not love things that are new? Well, when God returns and we are forever united with Him, there will be a new heaven and a new earth. The new heaven and new earth referred to is the Greek word *kaine*, meaning "new in character" or "fresh". Thus, this is not speaking about a new heaven where God will be enthroned, but an improved heaven and earth that will be replace the old.[31] In the Bible there are three different meanings to the word heaven. The first refers to the "blue sky" around us, our atmosphere. The second refers to the galaxy or the "night sky" and the third refers to the dwelling where God actually lives enthroned in glory.[32] Thus, this new heaven and new earth refers to the first definition of heaven. Not only will there be a new heaven and a new earth, but God will dwell among us. This is the greatest news of all. Through Jesus's sacrifice, we are united with Him. But that unity will be made fully complete as God dwells among us forever.

Next, let's look at the things that will pass away. No longer will there be any tears, death, mourning, crying, or pain. This is echoed in Revelation 7:17, as it says, "For the Lamb at the center of the throne will be their Shepherd; he will lead them to springs of living water. And God will wipe away every tear from their eye" (NIV). There will be no need for crying, for all will be made complete. In fact, all things will be made new and they "will stay new"[33]. Twice we see that God will lead us and give us water from the spring of the water of life. It does not cost us anything, and it will never cease to flow. This is the only water we will need, the water that is sourced in Christ.

God declares himself as Alpha and Omega, the Beginning and the End. Forevermore, God will reign and rule! Hallelujah!

---

[31] Guzik, "Revelation 21."
[32] Guzik, "Revelation 21."
[33] Guzik, "Revelation 21."

Week 4: Day 5

Read Revelation 22:1–5.

Check off the words and phrases that are used to describe the river of the water of life:

_____	Clear	_____	Rocky	_____	Stagnant
_____	Muddy	_____	Crystal	_____	Flowing

Notice the juxtaposition of the other words. The water of life that John describes is not muddy, stagnant, or growing with bacteria. Rather, it is crystal clear and flowing. This water of life is the same that was offered to the Samaritan woman back in John 4. It is the symbol of eternal life with Jesus. Observing these qualities of not just the water but the *river* of the water of life, we can understand and see the fullness that comes with life connected to God and the everlasting blessings that we receive when we believe in Him and allow Him to fill our thirst. Look back at the verses.

Where does the river flow through? _____

John tells us that the river flows directly through the middle of the city. What is the importance of the location of the river?

_____

_____

If the river flows in the middle of the city, it can be easily accessed by all people within that city. Thus, the eternal life and the everlasting blessings that are sourced by God the Father and Jesus are reached by all the people within the city. What stands on each side of the river?

_____

Does this tree sound familiar? If you said yes, then you would be correct (to rediscover this tree turn to Genesis 2:9). For, this is the same tree that Adam and Eve were forbidden to eat from. The tree of life is within heaven, standing tall on each side of the river. Because of Jesus's sacrifice and death on the cross, eternal life was made available to all who believe. In heaven, there will be no more evil and no more sin. When our eternity is secured with God, we will be able to eat and partake from the tree of life. This showcases the finality of our restoration.

What do you notice about the leaves of the tree of life, as described in Revelation 22:2?

_____

_____

These are not just ordinary leaves. These leaves hold healing power. However, in the original language, the word for healing here means "health-giving". It is the word in which we get our English word for therapeutic. The healing that the leaves hold will bring about a sense of well-being to the nations.[34] In heaven, there is hope, love, and unity. What in our nation needs to be healed? Pray that God will heal this very thing and look forward to the hope we have secured in heaven that one day there will be no more suffering among the nations.

What is the river's source? _____

The source of the river flows straight from the throne of God and the Lamb (who is Jesus). That is why, back in John 4, only Jesus could offer the woman at the well living water. Its source stems from Him and *only* Him. What does this mean for us? Our salvation and our eternal blessings stem from God the Father and Jesus alone. For only Jesus is the one true source. In John 14:6, it reads, "Jesus answered, 'I am the way and the truth and the life. No one comes to the Father except through me (NIV)". It is exclusively through Jesus that we can go to the Father. We see this visualized as we observe the river of the water of life. The only source is the Father and Jesus. Outside of Him, there is no access to eternal life. Although the world may offer vices for our thirsts, they will never be able to quench our thirst for eternal life.

Look back at Revelation 22:3–5.

---

[34] Guzik, "Revelation 22."

What is our role in heaven?

_____

_____

How long will we reign? _____

What can we learn from these verses?

_____

_____

As we close out the end of our study, I want us to fully feel this last connection. All along, we have discussed what happens when Jesus comes in and transforms our lives. We have talked about the salvation that is offered through Jesus alone. We have looked at the growth that must take place within our relationship with Jesus and the abundant blessings the Lord bestows upon those who love Him. This last week, we have been focusing on what heaven looks like and what it looks like for us as believers. I hope at the close of day 5, you have seen the hope that is secured for us and awaiting us in heaven. I hope you are filled with majesty and awe. From the end of our passage in Revelation 22, do not miss the fact that we will reign with the Lord Almighty and Jesus our Savior for ever and ever! We will need no one but the Lord. Even the light we need to see will be sourced in Him. Our rest, our shelter, and our daily bread will be sourced from the Lord. Let us take this and utilize this in our everyday life here on earth. For in God, we have all we need. He will meet our every need. He hears our every cry. He is our Lord God Almighty! We need no one else besides Him. This is the message Jesus gave to the woman at the well back in John 4. He knew her story; He knew the intimate and personal details. And yet He did not shame her. He gave her what she needed: life. Every need was met in Jesus alone. Rest and take hold of this truth. Only God will satisfy and fill our lives. Outside of God, we need nothing else. Accept the living water that He offers you.

1. What is your biggest takeaway from Week 4?

2. What verse or passage of Scripture was most meaningful to you?

3. What truth about God impacted you the most?

4. How can you practically apply what you learned this week into your day to day life?

_____

Notes:

NOTES

NOTES

NOTES

BIBLIOGRAPHY

Guzik, David. "1 Peter 3 – Submission and Suffering." Accessed October 26, 2020. https://enduringword. com/bible-commentary/1-peter-3/.

Guzik, David. "2 Kings 4 – God Works Miracles Through Elisha." Accessed October 16, 2020. https:// enduringword.com/bible-commentary/2-kings-4/.

Guzik, David. "Exodus 3 – Moses and the Burning Bush." Accessed October 14, 2020. https:// enduringword.com/bible-commentary/exodus-3/.

Guzik, David. "Exodus 17 – God's Provision and Protection of Israel." Accessed October 28, 2020. https://enduringword.com/bible-commentary/exodus-17/.

Guzik, David. "Genesis 6 – Man's Wickedness; God Calls Noah." Accessed October 11, 2020. https:// enduringword.com/bible-commentary/genesis-6/.

Guzik, David. "Hebrews 11 – Examples of Faith to Help the Discouraged." Accessed October 19, 2020. https://enduringword.com/bible-commentary/hebrews-11/.

Guzik, David. "Isaiah 12 – Words from a Worshipper." Accessed October 11, 2020. https://enduringword. com/bible-commentary/isaiah-12/.

Guzik, David. "Isaiah 55 – An Invitation to Receive the Glory of the Lord's Restoration." Accessed October 14, 2020. https://enduringword.com/bible-commentary/isaiah-55/.

Guzik, David. "Jeremiah 1 – The Call of a Reluctant Prophet." Accessed October 26, 2020. https:// enduringword.com/bible-commentary/jeremiah-1/.

Guzik, David. "Matthew 16 – Revealing who Jesus is and what He came to Do." Accessed October 28, 2020. https://enduringword.com/bible-commentary/matthew-16/.

Guzik, David. "Numbers 13 – Spies are Sent into Cannan." Accessed October 14, 2020.https://enduringword.com/bible-commentary/numbers-13/.

Guzik, David. "Numbers 14 – The People Reject Canaan." Accessed October 14, 2020.https://enduringword.com/bible-commentary/numbers-14/.

Guzik, David. "Revelation 21 – A New Heavens, a New Earth and a New Jerusalem." Accessed October 28, 2020.https://enduringword.com/bible-commentary/revelation-21/.

Guzik, David. "Revelation 22 – Come, Lord Jesus." Accessed October 22, 2020.https://enduringword.com/bible-commentary/revelation-22/.

Guzik, David. "Romans 8 – A New and Wonderful Life in the Spirit." Accessed October 19, 2020. https://enduringword.com/bible-commentary/romans-8/.

Henry, Matthew. "Jeremiah 1." Accessed October 28, 2020. https://www.biblestudytools.com/commentaries/matthew-henry-complete/jeremiah/1.html.

Spurgeon, H. Charles. "Psalm 23:1." Accessed October 13, 2020. https://www.biblestudytools.com/commentaries/treasury-of-david/psalms-23-1.html.

Spurgeon, H. Charles. "Psalm 23:4." Accessed October 13, 2020. https://www.biblestudytools.com/commentaries/treasury-of-david/psalms-23-4.html.

Spurgeon, H. Charles. "Psalm 65:2." Accessed October 16, 2020. https://www.biblestudytools.com/commentaries/treasury-of-david/psalms-65-2.html.

Spurgeon, H. Charles. "Psalm 65:3." Accessed October 16, 2020. https://www.biblestudytools.com/commentaries/treasury-of-david/psalms-65-3.html.

Spurgeon, H. Charles. "Psalm 65:6." Accessed October 16, 2020. https://www.biblestudytools.com/commentaries/treasury-of-david/psalms-65-6.html.

Spurgeon, H. Charles. "Psalm 84:1." Accessed October 19, 2020. https://www.biblestudytools.com/commentaries/treasury-of-david/psalms-84-1.html.

Spurgeon, H. Charles. "Psalm 84:2." Accessed October 19, 2020. https://www.biblestudytools.com/commentaries/treasury-of-david/psalms-84-2.html.

Spurgeon, H. Charles. "Psalm 84:6." Accessed October 19, 2020. https://www.biblestudytools.com/commentaries/treasury-of-david/psalms-84-6.html.

Spurgeon, H. Charles. "Psalm 116:13." Accessed October 11, 2020. https://www.biblestudytools.com/commentaries/treasury-of-david/psalms-116-13.

Printed in the United States
By Bookmasters